Squid-Tastic

Written by Michèle Dufresne

PIONEER VALLEY EDUCATIONAL PRESS, INC.

Splash! What just
swam by?
It was a squid!

Squid have a lot of **arms.**
Squid have gills
just like a fish,
but they are not fish.

Squid are mollusks, a group
of animals with soft bodies.
They live in oceans all
around the world.

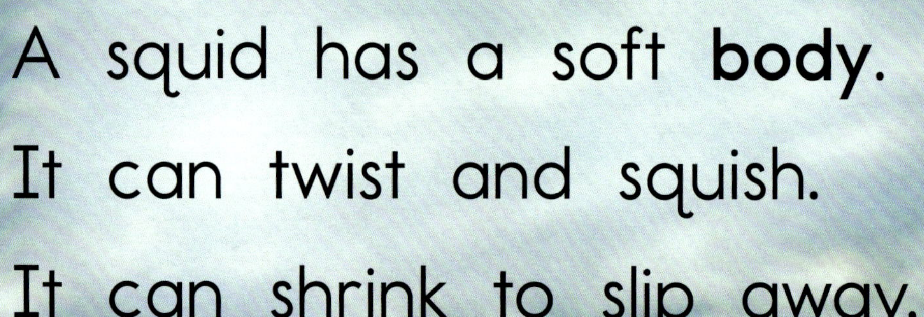

A squid has a soft **body**.
It can twist and squish.
It can shrink to slip away.

Though a squid's body is soft and squishy, its beak, which is in the center of its arms and tentacles, is incredibly hard.

Some squid are as big as a bus! But most are small.

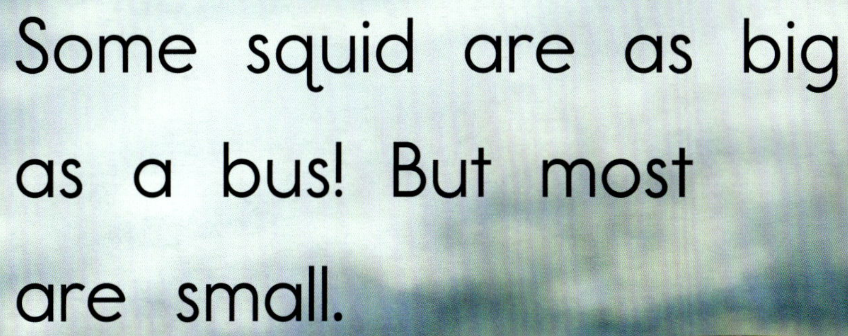

The colossal squid is the largest squid and can weigh up to 1,100 pounds! The smallest is the southern pygmy squid. It is less than one inch long.

Look out!

Here comes a **predator**!

Squid can swim fast.

With one big thrust,

the squid zips away.

A squid can also blend
in with rocks or send out
black ink. Splat!

When a squid feels scared, it shoots out
a cloud of ink. The dark ink hides the
squid so it can escape. The squid swims
away while the ink confuses its enemy.
Some squid will change color to blend
in with rocks and seaweed.

Squid hunt fish
and shrimp.
When they spot a fish,
they use their strong
tentacles to grab the fish.
Yum! Yum!

The tentacles and arms of a squid are not the same thing. Tentacles are longer and used to catch prey. Arms hold the prey after it has been caught.

If you spot a squid,
it can be a big thrill!

It is difficult to study giant squid because they live near the bottom of the ocean: 1,000 to 3,000 feet below the surface!

glossary

arms

body

predator

tentacles